5,10,16

ideals®
COUNTRY

MAY 2003

Dedicated to a celebration—through poetry and prose—of the American ideals of faith in God, loyalty to country, and love of family.

*Beyond my heart I need not reach
When all is summer there.
—John Vance Cheney*

In This Issue

IDEALS—Vol. 60, No. 3 May 2003 IDEALS (ISSN 0019-137X, USPS 256-240) is published six times a year: January, March, May, July, September, and November by IDEALS PUBLICATIONS, a division of Guideposts, 39 Seminary Hill Road, Carmel, NY 10512. Copyright © 2003 by IDEALS PUBLICATIONS, a division of Guideposts. All rights reserved. The cover and entire contents of IDEALS are fully protected by copyright and must not be reproduced in any manner whatsoever. Title IDEALS registered U.S. Patent Office. Printed and bound in USA by Quebecor Printing. Printed on Weyerhaeuser Husky. The paper used in this publication meets the minimum requirements of American National Standard for Information Sciences—Permanence of Paper for Printed Library Materials, ANSI Z39.48-1984. Periodicals postage paid at Carmel, New York, and additional mailing offices. POSTMASTER: Send address changes to Ideals, 39 Seminary Hill Road, Carmel, NY 10512. For subscription or customer service questions, contact Ideals Publications, a division of Guideposts, 39 Seminary Hill Road, Carmel, NY 10512. Fax 845-228-2115. Reader Preference Service: We occasionally make our mailing lists available to other companies whose products or services might interest you. If you prefer not to be included, please write to Ideals Customer Service.

ISBN 0-8249-1207-1 GST 893989236

Visit the *Ideals* website at www.idealsbooks.com

Cover: *The American Flag flutters in the summer breeze.*
Photo by Fred Sieb/H. A. Roberts.

Inside front cover: SUMMER DELIGHT *by artist D. Ison. Image from Arts Uniq.*

Inside back cover: *Brighton Beach by Edward Henry Potthast. Image from Christie's Images/SuperStock.*

Summer's Treasures

Louise Weibert Sutton

These are the jewels of summer: crystal dews,
Small emerald-tinted ferns, and hummingbirds
With ruby-colored throats; or sapphire lakes
Rippled by winds which bow the garnet rose;
Or bending, dancing, topaz marigolds
Which guard my flagstone path like sentinels,
Sunny and happy-faced the long days through.

These are the gems of sun, of breeze, of air:
Day's graceful butterflies on amber wings,
Rivers like ribbons set with amethysts,
And opalescent sunsets, touched with fire!
These are the treasured glories summer lends
Or gives to memory for heart's keepsake box:
Clover perfume, blue winds, and sudden song!

*Summer's treasures are gathered in a tidy garden in
Milwaukie, Oregon. Photo by Jessie Walker.*

June
Caroline Henning Bair

Come from the village across the green meadows,
Out where the woodland is bright with the flowers;
Gather an armful of misty pink roses,
Scatter their fragrance through June's sunny hours.

Let your heart sing with a silv'ry-winged bluebird,
Follow its flight where the white birches nod;
Rest in the clover and build for tomorrow,
Out where the hills are singing of God.

Through the soft twilight, return to the village;
Stars will be lighting the heavens' blue dome.
Sweetly the church bell will chime from the steeple,
Bidding you welcome to loved ones and home.

June Song
Barbara T. Grimes

Smooth rose petals on your cheek,
Roll in new-mowed mounds of hay,
Drift on currents down the creek,
Breathe in pearly morning day.
Stretch out under sun's sonata,
Sway with trees in easy rain,
Echo crickets' serenata;
You and June as one remain.

June's Manuscript
Marion R. Williams

The sixth month now submits her manuscript,
The first page scrolled with haloed daisy-wreath
And brier rose athwart a paragraph,
With fronded fern limned faintly underneath.
On beryl parchment greened by passing time,
June has inscribed her own exultant rhyme.

*Opposite: A rose garden in West Linn, Oregon, greets the
June morning. Photo by Dianne Dietrich Leis.*
*Overleaf: A garden bench anchors a profusion of purple
blooms in Eugene, Oregon. Photo by Dennis Frates.*

Devotions FROM THE Heart

Pamela Kennedy

For since the creation of the world God's invisible qualities—His eternal power and divine nature—have been clearly seen, being understood from what has been made, so that men are without excuse.
—Romans 1:20 (NIV)

SEEING IS BELIEVING

I had developed a friendship with a colleague; and although we had much in common, she didn't share my faith in God. We had engaged in some lively discussions about it, in which we remained cordial, but I was becoming increasingly frustrated. For every point I brought up about God's grace and mercy, she seemed to have a scientific or naturalistic explanation. I searched for information in magazines that I thought might appeal to her sense of logic, but even those didn't seem to convince her of the presence of a personal deity.

Then one night, we took a walk on a tropical reef at low tide. We picked our way through some tangled undergrowth, down a small, sandy bank to reach the exposed coral formation. Although the moon was full, we carried flashlights so we could peer into the tide pools in hopes of spying some of the nocturnal sea life lurking there. We walked carefully along the slippery ledge, concentrating on our footsteps and the beams of our lights. As we knelt over one of the pools, we noted three feathery blossoms waving gracefully in the clear water. A gentle touch with a stick, however, and these blossoms instantly retracted into small, white cylinders. They were sea worms, pulling their elaborate feeding apparatus back

into their shells. Farther along the edge of the pool we saw the bristly leg of a brittle star. Carefully coaxing it from its hold on the coral, we held it in our hands as it waved its scratchy legs, caught hold, and "walked" its way from finger to finger. Beautiful cowries, with shells as big as our fists, moved slowly along the submerged rocks while tiny hermit crabs scooted across the damp sand. Colorful anemones and dull sea cucumbers patiently filtered the algae-rich water, unbothered by our probing flashlights. Tiny minnows darted between rocky crevices, playing hide-and-seek with the silver moonbeams, and a baby octopus slipped his way between two pools, changing colors as he crossed bands of seaweed.

The nighttime reef was alive with myriad creatures, all apparently doing what they and their ancestors had been doing for ages. We paused, turned off our flashlights, and gazed up at the full

Thank You, God, for the intricate beauty of Your creation and the way it speaks to me about Your endless power and love.

moon, the wisps of clouds racing in the sky and the Belt of Orion twinkling in the tropical night. The musical swoosh of the lapping waves played background music to the palm branches sliding against one another in the wind. Suddenly, my friend whispered in an awe-filled voice, "There just has to be a God, don't you think?"

I was speechless. All my fine arguments, my logical presentations, shrank to emptiness beneath the eloquence of God's creation. I silently asked the Lord to forgive my arrogance in thinking I could somehow frame His majesty in words. And then I stood beside my friend and felt the hand of my Creator brush my cheek with a gentle breeze, and I whispered back, "There has to be."

Starfish and mussels line a tide pool on the Oregon Coast. Photo by Steve Terrill.

Pamela Kennedy is a freelance writer of short stories, articles, essays, and children's books. Wife of a retired naval officer and mother of three children, she has made her home on both U.S. coasts and currently resides in Honolulu, Hawaii.

Readers' Reflections

Readers are invited to submit original poetry for possible publication in future issues of IDEALS. Please send typed copies only; manuscripts will not be returned. Writers receive $10 for each published submission. Send material to Readers' Reflections, Ideals Publications, 535 Metroplex Drive, Suite 250, Nashville, Tennessee 37211.

My Garden
Lucille Wichern
Phoenix, Arizona

I wish I had a garden
In a quiet, woodsy spot
Where I could wander all alone
Without a worried thought.
Not a city garden
With plants all in a row,
But where each little flower
Could choose a place to grow.
A silver ribbon stream would
Be gently flowing there
Over pebbles washed and clean,
Without a worldly care.
While wandering in my garden,
I'd gather peace and love
To banish all frustrations
And lift my heart above.

Fireflies
Jean S. Craig
Danville, Virginia

If you watch the trees at night,
Also the lawn and hill,
You'll see the fireflies' little lights
When everything is still.

They flicker high above the trees
Like tiny fairy lights.
How magical it is to watch
On still and balmy nights.

I remember well my childhood,
When I would watch with glee;
For every little firefly
Was winking just for me!

And now that I am older,
It warms my heart to see
The busy little fireflies
Still blinking there for me.

Thoughts to Ponder

Doris V. Neumann
Buffalo, New York

I wandered through the woods today.
Warm earth cradled my feet;
Soft breezes gently kissed my face.
Oh, freedom felt so sweet.

I hoped the trees might understand
Thoughts running through my mind—
The laughter of the children
And the joys I left behind.

Wind rustled through their branches
As the leaves danced merrily
While sunbeams spread their cheery light
And filled my soul with glee.

I touched the trunks of birch trees,
Ran my fingers through the pine.

A maple leaf danced to my feet;
I knew the world was mine!

Beneath a weathered oaken stump
Forget-me-nots did nest;
As sunlight glistened through the trees
Nature portrayed her best.

It is within that sacred woods
Where heaven and nature meet
That God in wonderment and love
Lay blessings at my feet.

So here's my dearest wish to you
As twilight hours are nearing:
May God and nature condescend
To you within the clearing.

Fireflies

Jean Rugg Croft
Chattanooga, Tennessee

In early June, on balmy nights
They pierce the dark with blinking lights.
The air displays a magic show
As one by one their lanterns glow.
In grass-filled jars with punched-out lids
We'd catch and put those lampyrids.
Then watch upon our pillows soft
Wee flashlights turning on and off.

A Midsummer Night's Reverie

Jessie MacInnis
Elk Creek, Missouri

June bugs and bright fireflies
Dart through bush and brush.
Bats swoop low and stars come out
And softly sings the thrush.
Bullfrogs croak and crickets chirp
Their leggy serenades.
The breeze blows lightly as summer comes
And evening gently fades.

TWILIGHT MELODY

The twilight hours of dawn and sunset bring a song that is almost heavenly in nature. It is the ee-o-ay of the wood thrush, bringing the ultimate in bird music to my dooryard. This winged singer lights the day and welcomes the stars as darkness falls.

I am fortunate to have two woodlots near my door. I call them my cathedrals of music, for I can sit out-of-doors on these soft summer evenings, listening with awe and sensing the inspiring beauty of the chords deep within my heart.

As the thrushes sing, the fireflies flash their lights over the grass and bushes and trees. Sometimes I walk into the woods to be nearer to the bell-like tones. I can picture in my mind the richest of organs being played out there among the trees.

A century ago, F. Schuyler Matthews spoke in these terms of the wood thrush: "His music steals upon the senses like the opening notes of the great 'Fifth Symphony' of Beethoven; it fills one's heart with solemn beauty."

I receive inspiration from the devout song of the wood thrush. I feel like lifting my arms to the heavens in gratitude for the rich, rolling chords. He pours out his twilight melody to welcome the dawn, and then to close the curtains over the windows of the outdoor world at eventide.

The author of three books, Lansing Christman has contributed to Ideals *for almost thirty years. Mr. Christman has also been published in several American, international, and braille anthologies. He lives in rural South Carolina.*

A wood thrush checks her nest settled amongst the fallen leaves of a magnolia tree. Photo by Hal H. Harrison from Grant Heilman Photography, Inc.

White Clover
Ethel Barringer

Today, when I fashioned white clover
Into a wreath for a little girl's head,
Memory lit a bright candle
And beckoned my heart where she led.

Today, when I braided white clover,
There stretched a winding, green road;
My heart was softly singing
And it was walking tiptoed.

Today, when I fondled white clover,
There were myriad songs of the birds;
But they warbled only the music—
In my heart were the ecstatic words.

Boy and Clover
Lance Delaney

There was something strange about the clover
That made the small boy on the fence lean over,
As if by closeness he would understand
How this wide flood of green possessed the land,
These small round leaves that tumbled wave on wave
And this white blossom-foam that reached to lave
His feet. There was a sweetness to the feel
And coolness from bare toe to brown heel,
Making him certain that he must leap
And plunge in clover ankle-deep;
Then, as if strangeness had never been,
He knew clover was made for wading in.

A pasture of white clover invites bare feet and makers of clover neck-laces. Photo by Peter Dean from Grant Heilman Photography, Inc.
Inset: White Clover. Photo by Jessie Harris.

Summer Kids

Catherine Calvert

If there is a season that summons childhood, surely it is summer. One sniff of new-cut grass, and I slip through the trapdoor of time to the last days of school, when the air hung heavy as a math book and the rumble-mumble of the mower filled the classroom with the promise of the months stretching before us. Summer was freedom—soft shoes, bare knees, simple suppers, and tag in the twilight. Even now, amid days of duties and years filled with plans and promptings, summer awakens the child in me—bare feet in the green grass, chasing after fireflies. And the years that have passed seem as ephemeral as dandelion down.

Who doesn't remember how the early sun made staying in bed impossible, especially when the birds were clamoring? When I slip on my sneakers I am nine again, impatient with my tangled sheets and ready to tiptoe past the sleepers, out the door. The dew turns the tips of my Keds sodden as I walk, directionless, but searching for signs of summer at its crest. Hollyhocks hold up their rough stems and furled flowers. Mint leaps green and fresh by the house, ready for the iced tea in the fridge. Birds swoop and call, threading their cries like ribbons in the air. Here in the garden, a world wakes, one so easy to brush by on the way to something else. But for a child, world enough and, yes, time enough to be squandered. How tempting to know that breakfast can last for hours outdoors under the trees or be a scooped-up handful of berries and crust of bread, carried along as you wander.

Do you remember the childhood feeling of being half asleep, lulled by breezes and buzzes, yet at the same time aware of the vivid life around you? To bring it back, try a hammock, shared with a child, some lemonade, and a lapful of books. In a sweep or two, tomorrow and yesterday disappear, and the only anxieties are whether or not the bee will land on a bare toe and how fast the ice will melt.

Summer is a great leveler between parent and child. When I sink into a hammock with my youngest, we nap, browse, talk, equals in our eternal afternoon. As I watch the sun strike rainbows in her hair and hold a hand over her eyes as she dozes, our rocking takes me back to the porch swing at my grandmother's, where I swung, one toe on the stones, head on the rose-strewn pillows, books around me, sure that this was life. Discovering the child in oneself means recapturing the certainty that, sometimes, doing nothing is doing something.

Take exploring. It can mean looking hard at what's right in front of you, perhaps turning over the dirt in the garden to see what comes wiggling out. The best companion for this activity is a toddler, who'll squat absorbed, reaching for a worm, poking a finger at the curious bugs—"Do they pinch?" And sometimes it takes a higher perch. The world from the crotch of the apple tree has a beauty worth climbing for. As a child, I loved the feeling of being hidden up there, known only to a bird or two, until I gave myself away by dropping crab apples on my brother's head. Recently I climbed a tree again, and there it all was—the rhythm of the branches and the supple sway of the tree, the way the leaves shattered the sunshine into dancing shadows while I, silent, watched the world.

Summer's freedom has its own flavors: water-

A toddler runs along a country road in rural North Carolina. Photo by ImageState/Bob Schatz.

melon from the farm stand and suppers that are just a matter of boiling water for the fresh-picked corn and slicing some tomatoes. It's the season for impromptu desserts, for chasing the drips down the cone or slicing the red strawberries and pouring the cream. It's finally baking that pie, the one with all the nutmeg, when the peaches arrive. Has anyone ever had too many strawberries or peaches, or too many blueberries eaten from the bucket while perched on a stone wall? Even ice pops, in colors nature never knew, have their place. Children build memories of such feasts, savored amid sun and sand and salt air with the hoots of seagulls in the background. We have only to salt the fries and shoo the gulls and we're there again, feeding hungers that have nothing to do with the menu.

Sometimes there's the wild, outdoor hunger to run again, as children do—across the sand, the sidewalks, the fields, to race into the cold shock of ocean water that casts lacy foam on the sand. Instead, grown, we shop for the supper, warn of sand in the sheets and too many ice creams, book the beach house, schedule the swimming lessons, pick out the splinters. But it still remains, that special preserve of summer, its call heard with the first bird, the snap of a screen door, the susurration of the maple trees at evening. And that other sound heard from my childhood, as we were called to our beds by our mothers after careening through the gathering darkness in a game of hide-and-seek. "All-ee, all-ee, come-in-free," sang out the child who was It. And we ran towards home, coming in free indeed.

Reflection

June Masters Bacher

How haunting that where I may be
A constant shadow follows me.
I'm careful not to go astray—
My shadow'd go the self-same way.
I cannot from his presence flee;
And what I do, he does like me.
When I stand up straight and tall,
My straight-up shadow on the wall,
I dare not stumble—he will fall.
He must think my image fine,
For he reflects me line by line.
I must remember as I go
Through summer sun and winter snow,
As seasons pass me one by one,
My shadow lengthens—
He's my son.

Two Shadows on the Wall

Craig E. Sathoff

Throughout the years I still recall
Two shadows on my small son's wall.
By mellow rays of one dim light
I read the boy to sleep each night.

We made a mural plain to see,
The shadows of my son and me.
The shadow of the one was small,
A wispy little lad, not tall.

He leaned against the other one,
His meeting with the day now done.
The larger shadow tossled there
A curly head of golden hair.

They folded hands and said a prayer
To thank the One who blessed them there.
Two shadows on my small son's wall,
And peace and love reigned over all.

A young boy dreams peacefully.
Photo by Barry Elz/ImageState.

A MESSAGE TO FATHERS

Grace Noll Crowell

Bear it in mind that to your sons, O men,
You stand as idols in their boyish breasts.
They watch you with appraising eyes, and when
You speak or move, their attitude attests
Their admiration for you, their desire
To grow more like you, these dear watching ones!
O fathers, let it be a burning fire
Within you that you may not fail these sons.

Take God for your advisor through the days;
Make Him your companion and your guide,
And thus you will be fitted for the ways
Of fatherhood. The troubled world is wide,
And there is need of men. No greater task
Could any man be called upon to do;
No higher privilege the heart could ask
Than this which God Himself allotted you:
To rear your sons, to keep their faith, then send
Them forth to serve a hurt world torn by strife.
Oh, give them early the risen Christ as friend,
And you will give them more, much more than life.

The greatest profession in the world
is that of being a father.
—Author Unknown

MORNING SHAVE by Richard Hook. Image from Ideals Publications.

21

Ten Rosy Fingers

Jessie Wilmore Murton

He built a wall about his heart
And thought that none could scale its height,
Then smiled serenely at the world
And went his way with footsteps light.

But one there came, with toddling steps,
And stopped beside the wall to play.
Ten rosy fingers picked the lock
And stole that guarded heart away!

To a Young Father

Edith G. Schay

Seize these golden hours
Of laughter with your son,
And lock them safely in your heart
Till childhood days are done.

Then you will remember
Your baby's smile and frown;

His small round head, his tiny hands,
His eyes of shining brown.

Seize these golden hours
Of laughter while you can.
Soon, too soon, your little boy
Will be a full-grown man.

TIME WITH DAD by Steve Hanks. Image from Hadley House.

The Water Jug

Mildred Perl Van Horn

It was a long, long time ago
When I was a child and time was slow.
My father worked in the fields all day,
And there wasn't much extra time for play.
The dusty field was my magic rug
When I carried water in an earth-brown jug.
I dawdled along in the cornfield dust,
But always thrilled at my father's trust.
For every day at half-past ten
He'd raise his eyes and see me again—
Just halfway there on my magic rug,
And he'd wait for a drink from my earth-brown jug.

COTSWOLD FARM by Josephine Trotter. Image from SuperStock.

Old Hammers and Old Saws

Evelynn Merilatt Boal

Old hammers and old saws
remind me of him—
his hands, all gnarled and calloused
from years of driving nails
and handling wood.

I see old tools everywhere;
sometimes they are hung on walls,
ceiling to floor. Braces and bits,
hammers and saws, chisels, files
and planes. He used them all.

I loved to watch him plane a two-by-four.
His strokes were strong and sure.
There would be long coils of thin wood strewn about the floor.
I'd put them in my hair, and
pretend I had long curls.

My dad's been gone a long, long time.
But memories spring fresh whenever
I see old tools—old hammers
and old saws.

VILLAGE CARPENTER by Edward Henry Potthast.
Image from Christie's.

God's Helper

S. Omar Barker

The day that he turned eighty-two,
Grandfather had a job to do—
A special job that could not wait,
Lest some tomorrow be too late.
Slow were his movements but content
His heart, as to the task he bent
Of setting out new apple trees—
Six slender stalks. Upon old knees
He knelt to place young roots with care,
Whose fruiting he would never share.
Some day a child he'd never know
Would wander down the shaded row,
Some star-eyed girl, some lusty boy,
To share his apples—and his joy.
Old men who plant young apple trees—
The whole world leans on such as these!

A row of apple trees in Oregon waits to share its bounty. Photo by Dennis Frates.

The Yarn Spinner
Alice B. Johnson

Intent on every word, the small boy hears
A story woven of an old man's years
That with the telling finds a space to grow
In splendor for a boy who wants it so.
And as the wondrous tale unravels,
Along an old-world trail a small boy travels,
A boy who hangs upon each chosen word,
As with the spinning yarn the air is stirred,
Until the hero worshiper is led,
His hand held fast in grandfather's, to bed.

Great-Grandpa's Fun
Beatrice Branch

I didn't have the costly toys
You children seem to need,
Yet there were many things to do
And shelves of books to read.

With my old dog I climbed each hill,
Explored each rocky nook,
And fished for darting shiny trout
While wading in a brook.

I swung from trapeze rings above
Cool sawdust in the shed,
And learned to build a skipper
Long before I had a sled.

I climbed on rafters in the barn
And jumped into the hay
And sometimes helped to drive the mare
To town on market day.

The simplest pleasures of my youth
Are lost, beyond a doubt,
Since I enjoyed all kinds of fun
That you don't know about.

STORIES OF A LIFETIME by Dave Barnhouse.
Image from Hadley House.

31

THROUGH MY WINDOW

BEACHED
Pamela Kennedy

When I was little, trips to the beach were a regular feature of summer. We didn't live close to the ocean, so our beach was the shore of a small lake. Mom made a picnic supper of potato salad and fried chicken, and as soon as Daddy got home from work, we headed out. It was a treat to eat outside in the long, daylight-saved summer evenings, and the best part was that at the beach my parents would play. Daddy did headstands, Mom went down the big steel water slide, and we all splashed in the water together. Now that I live in a place surrounded by beaches, I've come to realize that this experience wasn't one limited to my 1950s childhood. There's something about the beach that brings out the child in just about everyone.

Just last week, I went to the beach with my twenty-four-year-old son and a friend of his. We took all the sensible things one should take: towels, beach chairs, sunblock, hats, and books to read. And then we tossed the boogie boards, the foam football, and the Frisbee in the back of the van. Once we arrived and chose a place to drop our stuff, we were off and running into the water, looking for the perfect wave. Unless you're in competition or trying to impress someone, form doesn't matter much at the beach. Anyway, I find it difficult to get too serious about something with a name like "boogie board." You basically stand in waist-high water, waiting for a wave to come by. When it's just beginning to break, you flop on your board, facing the beach, and hang on. If you've done it right, the wave picks you up and rushes you toward the shore with exhilarating speed. It's hard not to laugh out loud. You stop by rolling off in the sand, getting dumped by a second wave, or, if you have some degree of technique, by turning

The Test
Isabelle F. Duncanson

Now who can measure me a summer day?
Would you take cups of sunshine gleaming bright
Or pints of children's laughter as they play?
You think a yard of meadow would be right?

A test like this you could not help but fail.
You cannot grasp the quantity nor size,
Nor estimate, nor measure on your scale,
The gifts that God has spread before our eyes.

Summer Vignette
Dan A. Hoover

Unblemished blue of sun-gold skies,
Fresh flowers, skimming butterflies,
Child-happy swimming pool and park,
Fireflies to chase with velvet dark.
Dusk whippoorwills whose plaintive calls
Wrap mystery around it all,
As nature hums a carefree tune
To pace sweet summer afternoon.

Coneflowers and daisies mingle beautifully in a field in Alden, Illinois. Photo by Jessie Walker.

35

July

Della Adams Leitner

July's a matron with her growing brood;
    The dreams of spring still linger in her eyes.
    Mature in beauty, fashioned by the wise
And tender joys of loving motherhood.

Perfection is the ideal of her art
    That reaches for completeness in the days
    Of warmth provided by the virile rays
The lavish sun releases as his part.

So when her course is done, she leaves in store
    The sustenance of fields and gardens fair,
    That from her plenty each may have a share;
Maternal care sees all provided for.

What legacy of foresight July gives,
And when the winter comes her memory lives.

July

Margaret Rorke

July is a soldier saluting his flag;
So proud of his country he's given to brag
'Bout all of her virtues, her wisdom, her lore:
A swain to the lady he's come to adore.

July can relax in his own summer sun,
Completely ignoring what ought to be done.
He relishes picnics and ball games and such;
Vacations and gard'ning he likes very much.

July, as a person, is youth at high time,
Developing fully but not at his prime.
He's vibrant, warm-hearted, and eager to try.
Life's harvest is still but a gleam in his eye.

A luncheon under the trees offers a stunning summer view of Sturgeon Bay, Wisconsin. Photo by Jessie Walker.

Know'st Thou America

Victor E. Southworth

Know'st thou America,
    where we from every land
Unite in friendly fellowship,
    all evil to withstand?
Where freedom of the people
    forever reigns supreme?
Where we together labor
    to render real our dream?

Know'st thou America?
    We call the world to see
The greatness of America
    that is and is to be.
Know'st thou the glory of what
    we can achieve
When we for one another
    in liberty believe?

When Human worth stands foremost,
    the chiefest of all good,
And democratic principle
    is clearly understood?
Know'st thou America?
    With spirit unconfined
In joyous self-surrender
    we stand for humankind!

*Geraniums and flags fill an old wagon
with color in Tilton, New Hampshire.
Photo by William H. Johnson.*

Pattern for the Flag

Bessie Saunders Spencer

I saw the sky with white and crimson bars;
Its dull-blue dome still held the sparkling stars.
Perhaps once, long ago, someone passed by
And saw this vivid pattern in the sky.
I hope they read in it a sacred sign
And planned and made our flag from God's design.

Keeper of the Free

Lori Shannon

Drifting gently in the air
With eagle and with cloud,
The flag, with majesty and grace,
Flies jubilant and proud.

Her pride is in pastoral scenes
Touched pink by blooming day;
The pond at twilight and the wave,
The white of winter's play;

The echoes of brave words once said
By those who died for dreams,
Whose sacrifice became the source
From which her triumph streams.

Because they lived and died for her
With resolution true,
Her role as guardian of the free
Will live forever new.

*An American flag proudly waves outside a home in
Bristol, New Hampshire. Photo by William H. Johnson.*

Ring Out,
Sweet Freedom Bell!

Herman T. Roberts

Ring out! Ring out, sweet freedom bell!
Ring out our nation's noblest theme.
Ring out and let thy tolling swell
The joyful triumph of her dream.

Ring out the pilgrims' yearning quest,
Whose vision shaped our destiny,
Bold patriots now long at rest
Whose courage gave us liberty.

Through village streets and homes and hearts,
Through farms and cities send thy peal,
And may the message it imparts
Renew our patriotic zeal.

For Stars and Stripes, floats, and bands
Reliving Independence Day,
For those, still ruled by tyrants' hands,
Who think of us and yearn and pray.

Ring out the voices of the soul,
The vision and the will to share;
Ring out again, sweet bell, and toll
The hope of freedom everywhere!

The majestic Teton Range is reflected in a tranquil pond. Photo by Terry Donnelly.

Flag Song

Lydia Avery Coonley Ward

Out on the breeze,
O'er land and seas,
A beautiful banner is streaming;
Shining its stars,
Splendid its bars,
Under the sunshine 'tis gleaming.
Hail to the flag,
The dear, bonny flag—
The flag that is red, white, and blue.

Over the brave
Long may it wave,
Peace to the world ever bringing,
While to the stars
Linked with the bars
Hearts will forever be singing.
Hail to the flag,
The dear, bonny flag—
The flag that is red, white, and blue.

Children offer a patriotic prayer in artist Donald Zolan's orginal oil painting entitled FAITH IN AMERICA. Copyright © Zolan Fine Arts, LLC. Ridgefield, Connecticut. All rights reserved.

A Nation's Strength
Ralph Waldo Emerson

Not gold, but only man can make
    A people great and strong;
Men who, for truth and honor's sake,
    Stand fast and suffer long.

Brave men who work while others sleep,
    Who dare while others fly—
They build a nation's pillars deep
    And lift them to the sky.

The Opportunity
Gail Brook Burket

The land where freedom breathed her first pure breath
Revealed man's right to rule, when tyrants scourged
Mankind. The people broke the bands of death
Oppressing them, and Lazarus-like emerged.
The sons of freedom, called American,
In earth's lone citadel of liberty,
Showed wonders could be wrought, when common man
Lives unencumbered by old tyranny.

Here Pilgrim faith in God and man became
The cornerstone on which our fathers reared
A nation that would hold a beacon flame
For all who followed where they pioneered.
Their valiant lives have let the whole earth see
A glimpse of man's potentiality.

The Maroon Bell Peaks stretch into the clouds above Colorado's Crater Lake. Photo by Londie G. Padelsky.

WHEN TRAIL'S END WAS ONLY THE BEGINNING

Jay Scriba

Today's family vacationers take their summer house with them—a bus, trailer, truck camper, or tent. Like driven refugees, they race from campground to turnout, frantically collecting scenic views, bumper stickers, and sand from crowded beaches.

It's fun, of course, after a year stuck in town. Yet some of the Depression generation must dream wistfully of all the quiet, comfortable old log cabins and cottages now gathering moss. Every family had one—rented or inherited—that they returned to year after year. . . .

Late afternoon found you in the cutover around Pelican Lake. Then, at sunset, you bumped down the last sandy logging road and there it was— Camp Trail's End, a red tarpaper shack, neat with white battens, a peeled jack-pine flagpole, and Uncle Jake's whitewashed old duck skiff, now full of tiger lilies.

Kids always dashed down the hill and out on the dock for a first look at the clear, green waters of Lake Dorothy. While Dad pried off the nailed shutters—swearing once again that he would find a better way in the fall—your mother hunted the key (always hung inside a floor joist, three studs to the left of the door) and snapped open the big railroad switch lock.

The hand pump in the kitchen had to be primed, the kerosene stove filled, the flypaper strung up, the rag rugs shaken, and the Flit gun sprayed vigorously to discourage flies that had crept through the rusty screens.

Old cottages always smelled, but pleasantly— of a generation of woodsmoke, bacon grease, oil of citronella, and mildewed mohair armchairs damp from the spring's roof leaks.

After a quick supper—homemade sauerkraut and wieners, with maybe a dish of raspberries picked in the woods—there was just time for a boy to make a few casts from shore, hurling a red and white Bass-Oreno with his new Sears Roebuck telescopic steel casting rod. (Spinning reels and fiberglass were still a war away.) Inevitably there was a hopeless backlash to unsnarl—picking with a crochet needle in the glow of the bare light bulb.

Then it was off to bed, to wheeze asthmati-

Old cottages always smelled, but pleasantly—of a generation of woodsmoke . . .

---

cally under woolen army blankets before falling asleep at last.

Next morning you awoke to rain; gray, slicing sheets that drummed on the stove, dripping down to streak rust on the iron barrel stove.

But soon there were fat pine knots popping in the stove and pancakes on the table, with the big blue enamel coffee pot exhaling clouds of pungent glory.

What to do with an all-day soaker and whitecaps on the lake? A kid could rummage in the bookshelf for the book he'd been reading last Labor Day—*Tom Swift and His Skyship*, *Billy Whiskers*, *The Bobbsey Twins at the Farm*. He and his sister could play "Old Maid" or get out the jigsaw puzzle of the moose and hunter—the box carefully marked "five pieces missing" so you wouldn't go crazy looking for pieces to complete the waterfall behind the moose.

There was a windup Victrola, the kind with

the big megaphone horn, that scratched hints of music from records labeled "Ukulele Lady," "K-K-K-Katy," "Pack Up Your Troubles in Your Old Kit Bag," and "There's a Long, Long Trail A'Winding."

Your mother gazed out the steaming windows, planning an expedition after balsam and sweet fern to stuff the pillows she had embroidered all winter.

Your father and Uncle Ivan eyed the horseshoe pit, calculating that by evening the wind might lay enough to seine minnows and try for a mess of walleyes off Link's Point. After twenty-five years, they knew every sandbar and weed bed in the lake and just where to get the "lunkers" whose gaping, snaggletoothed heads were nailed to trees around the fish-cleaning bench. And they caught lots of real eating fish, deep-fried to tawny lightness and eaten with rings of Bermuda onions drenched in pepper sauce.

A dad and his sons enjoy a summer day of fishing in a cool lake.

That night, you fell to dead, snoring sleep, with a loon calling on the foggy lake. Then, how glorious to awaken at seven in the morning to sunlight pouring through a crack in the eaves, the sight of the blue lake through a grove of white birches.

What to do on a morning when Oneida County has become a paradise of clear skies, soft air, and earthy woodsy smells? There were scratchy, wool bathing suits to dig out, embarrassingly holed despite the reeking mothballs in the steamer trunk.

There was a cold, shocking plunge down to the bright gravel of the cove beach, reveling in the freshness of rainwater. There were pudgy, black bluegills to catch, yanked from under the lily pads with a cane pole, cork bobber, and pink curl of night crawler. . . .

Nobody ever thought of barbecuing or even eating outdoors, except for a bag lunch taken to the raspberry bramble or the blueberry patch.

It was a big treat, in this day before drive-ins, when Uncle Ivan drove to town for the makings of "Black Cow" sundaes—root beer and vanilla ice cream. It was an adventure when, maybe twice a summer, you borrowed a pickup truck and horsed a boat into Sweeny Lake, sworn to hold the world's record muskie. ("Chet Boynton says the conservation boys netted it through the ice in 1928—seventy-four pounds!")

And so it went in those simple, peaceful days of lanterns, waves lapping against the dock, a phoebe nesting in the woodshed, a black iron skillet frying perch to a crispness unknown to Teflon.

Sure, it got a little old by Labor Day. But like today, you remembered the good things, the rain on the roof, the laughter beyond the bedroom door curtain, and the hoot of the Flambeau 400 pounding north through the dark forest for Ashland and Lake Superior.

Patterns of a Nation

Margaret A. Welton

My home, it is built in the land of the free,
Where brooks in green meadows
    meet the tides of the seas;
Where snowcapped mountains are lost in the clouds
And blanketed over with pine needle shrouds;
Where wilderness, canyons, and uncharted terrain
Stretch from sunrise to sunset in beauty untamed.

My home is the valley, snug and secure,
To the leeward of granite peaks, proud and demure;
Sheltered from north winds, sunny and warm
Where joy in mere living, each hour is reborn.
My home is built strong on foundation of stone,
Set deep in the black soil
    from whence good things come.

Roots of a good life have captured my soul,
For this is my homeland. This is my own—
Each moist grain of soil; each soft blade of grass;
Trout in the hill stream; the snow on the pass;
Deer in the thicket; the vast upland range;
Each flower, each crevice; the splattering rain.

This is my heritage, my pride, my hope.
My name is American! This land is my own.

My home, it is built on the land of the free
Where the vast rolling plains
    stretch for miles endlessly;
Where coarse prairie grass gently sways to and fro,
Scorched in the summer heat, buried in snow.

My home is the great plain, relentless, huge;
Filled with a sameness and dark earthy hues.
I love it, wouldn't change it.
Every inch of this prairie I call my own—
The dust that nigh chokes me;
    the sweat on my brow;
The purple sage, rattlesnakes, prairie dogs, storms;

The thunder that rumbles, echoes, resounds
From horizon to horizon with unearthly sound;
Azure skies, blaze-crested clouds at sundown,
Then darkness, stars twinkling down;
Spine-tingling howls of coyotes at night;
Sparks from a campfire dancing far out of sight;

Lowing of cattle, and silence, like death;
A vast land, a lonely land, but I love it best.
This is my heritage, my pride, my hope.
My name is American! This land is my own.

Red poppies dance under a summer sky in Teton County, Idaho. Photo by Terry Donnelly.

55.

HANDMADE HEIRLOOM

PAINTED FLOORCLOTH

Melissa Lester

From the start, I knew Charlene and I would be friends. Both newcomers to a metropolitan area and large church, we were feeling unsettled and anonymous when we met. We shared feelings of homesickness; together we looked for new doctors, dentists, and dry cleaners. As we established our homes, we found a special friendship. We are always quick to offer a listening ear, a pot of soup, or babysitting as needed.

Now, Charlene and her family will be moving again—into a cramped apartment in a distant city. I wanted to give Charlene something to remember our friendship and the wonderful times we've had together. I decided to make her a painted floorcloth, which I hope will be the perfect gift to brighten Charlene's new kitchen.

About three hundred years ago, floorcloths became an inexpensive substitute for other, more expensive floorcoverings. The British copied the patterns of painted wall hangings and table runners of fifteenth-century France onto coverings for their unfinished wood floors. These floorcloths were made of heavy canvas that had been stretched and sized. Historically referred to as *oylcloths*, they were later called "crumb cloths" because of their popular use in the dining room, but were also used in parlors and hallways.

Homeowners often painted a floorcloth with simple geometric designs. Others hand-painted or stenciled more elaborate designs; and some replicated the patterned marble floors of the day. As the designs became more complex, and the floorcloths more popular, the trade expanded in early eighteenth-century England. By the end of the century, the manufacturing of floorcloths was a thriving industry. Looms used to make sailcloth were employed to make the widths necessary to seamlessly cover large rooms, and hand-held wooden blocks were used to stamp the cloths with patterns inspired by wallpapers, pavement patterns, and even woven carpets.

In America, settlers initially imported floorcloths from England; but these were expensive, and their journey across the sea meant they often arrived in poor condition. After the American Revolution, the demand for American-made domestic goods increased, and colonial painters and artisans began building their own floorcloth businesses. In the beginning, available raw materials resulted in cruder textiles; but soon the

> *To a friend's house, the road is never long. —Dutch proverb*

quality of American-made floorcloths rivaled English goods.

Painted floorcloths were used in homes both grand and small. Many were highly prized possessions, often mentioned in wills and featured prominently in family portraits.

The introduction of linoleum in 1860 brought the end of the once booming floorcloth industry. But a century later, the art form was revived by artisans eager for a return to a simpler way of life. Folk artists began to paint floorcloths with bold colors and familiar forms. In the years since, interest in historic preservation has led many artisans to replicate patterns of old. Today's floorcloths, made by artisans and novices alike, showcase a wide range of artistic styles.

To make a painted floorcloth, you will need to build a wooden frame the size of your desired finished piece. Sketch out a design and determine the colors you want to use. You can also use stencils for your design. Purchase a piece of heavy canvas six inches larger on all four sides than the desired finished size. (Cotton canvas will shrink, so keep this in mind when measuring.) Wash the canvas to remove any sizing; stretch and staple it to the wooden frame. Brush shellac evenly on one side of the canvas.

A painted floorcloth softens a wooden floor. Photo by Jessie Walker.

(Note: Shellac is flammable. Always work outdoors and away from any open flame.) After the first side has dried, brush shellac on the other side and let it dry completely.

Paint your floorcloth with acrylic paints, following your design or stencils; let the cloth dry thoroughly. Once dry, brush on several coats of shellac. This will help the floorcloth withstand foot traffic, and give the finished design a more mellow, aged look. After a few days, cut the floorcloth from the frame. The edges can be left alone, bound, or folded under and sealed with contact cement.

The floorcloth I am making for Charlene will reflect the warm tones and fruit motifs she favors. A base coat of burgundy will provide a lovely background for green and golden pears and sage green leaves. I'll finish off the pattern with fine black outlines and accents in cream and metallic gold. On her moving day, I'll carefully lay an old, clean sheet over the floorcloth, roll it up carefully, with the design-side in, and present the floorcloth as a going away present.

The completed floorcloth will infuse Charlene's new kitchen with color. But it will also, I hope, keep close the loving memories of her friends. As Charlene unpacks and settles into her new home, she will smile when she sees her new painted floorcloth and know that, from across the miles, it's my way of rolling out the red carpet of friendship and of saying "welcome home."

Found: Lost Youth

Evelyn R. Liddell

If you should walk
Down any country lane
And sip a stalk of mellow sugar cane;
If you fling stones
Across a startled brook
Or gather cones
In a fragrant piny nook;
Then you will see
Yourself, a boy, at play
And must agree
You found lost youth that day.

Summer's Mirror

Judy Barnes

A thousand summers ago
on warm star-specked nights
we captured fireflies,
imprisoned them in Mason jars
for make-believe lanterns.

A thousand summers ago
when days stretched endlessly,
we splashed in the creek
where water wore rocks satin-smooth
and turned skin cold white.

A thousand summers ago
as clocks ticked just for fun,
we spent blanket hours
spotting creatures in floating clouds,
giggling with each other.

For delicious summers past
and all those yet to come,
a lemonade toast
in praise of childhood freedom
and grown-up reflection.

A Special Place

Susan M. Nehrbass

My secret place, when I was a child,
Was a clearing set on the side of a hill,
A pasture overgrown and wild,
But it was mine and beautiful.
The Indian grass there grew waist-high,
Dull gold in the lazy afternoon.
I could make a nest and watch the sky
Till shadows warned of dinner soon.

The jack pines stood to see me go.
Whistling the dog from his rabbit chase,
I always knew they would point me home
And keep their watch on my secret place.
I wonder if someone has built a house
And cut the grass and chopped the pine.
Or has the clearing stayed as it was,
Lonely and friendly and somehow mine?

A small stream wanders through the grasses in Grand Teton National Park. Photo by Terry Donnelly.

Fieldstone Fence

Ralph W. Seager

His field lay clogged, and long before
His plow could stir the sunlight in
He had to stack the scattered store
Of rocks that wore this acre thin.

He built this fence of quiet peace
Which never fortified this land
Or said the neighbor's world must cease
Exactly where these rift-rocks stand.

Now chipmunks flick along its shelves
Where mosses hush the splintered stones,
And hermit thrushes dare themselves
To try their treble double-tones.

No barrier in length or height,
But a resting place when feet may falter.
These fieldstones built a fence, all right—
I think they nearly raised an altar.

Rock Walls: Connecticut

Thelma Finefrock

I did not see the hands that laid them here
    To mark the lines and make the cattle lane.
Those hands are part of earth and atmosphere
    But walls they built with care remain
To ease my labor, make my days serene,
    To serve as summer tightropes for my girls,
And, when the snow lies heaped and curving clean,
    For use as runs and landing strips by squirrels.
I'd like to know his name, but on my deed
    It's not recorded when he tilled these lands.
To know that he was here, I've all I need;
    He's present perfect where each rock wall stands.

*Opposite: Rhododendron blossoms crown a stone wall in
Hardwick, Massachusetts. Photo by William H. Johnson.*

ROBERT FROST

Nancy J. Skarmeas

In 1893, nineteen-year-old Robert Frost, in a letter to his future wife Elinor White, declared his intention to become a poet. The announcement was not met with great celebration by Elinor, nor by Frost's friends and family, who wondered if young Rob, having already dropped out of Dartmouth College, might pursue a more practical path. But Frost was resolute; he would be a poet.

I'm going out to clean the pasture spring;
I'll only stop to rake the leaves away

Of course, we know that the story ends happily: Frost become a successful poet, but this happened neither overnight nor simply. More than twenty years would pass before the self-confident young man with a gift for verse would became the publicly recognized poet.

(And wait to watch the water clear, I may):
I sha'n't be gone long.—You come too.

Frost, the poet of New England, was born a continent away in San Francisco in 1874, but his family's roots were in Massachusetts. That is where his mother, Isabelle Moody Frost, moved her family after her husband's death in 1885. Frost attended school in Lawrence, Massachusetts, and graduated from Lawrence High School in 1892, sharing valedictory honors with Elinor White.

I'm going out to fetch the little calf
That's standing by the mother. It's so young,

In the two decades following high school,

Frost's path wandered and stalled and wandered again. He worked as an elementary school teacher, as an actor's manager, in a woolen mill, and as a journalist. After he and Elinor married and started a family, Frost gave college studies a second try at Harvard, but did not stay a full year. He then tried his hand at farming and found that he loved farm life; but when he could not support his growing family through farming, he returned again to teaching. All the while, however, poetry kept hold of his heart.

It totters when she licks it with her tongue.
I sha'n't be gone long.—You come too.

Frost found that his poetry flowed naturally and abundantly within the demands of farm life; but farming did not support his family. He found teaching both challenging and fulfilling; but the intellectual demands and busy schedule left little room for his poetry to flourish. By 1912, Robert Frost had reached a crossroads. He was thirty-eight years old, a husband, and a father. He had found a niche as a teacher at a college of education and

NAME: Robert Lee Frost

BORN: San Francisco, March 26, 1894

ACCOMPLISHMENTS: Pulitzer Prize for Poetry, 1924, 1931, 1937, 1943.

MARRIED: Elinor White

EDUCATION: Attended Dartmouth College and Harvard University

DIED: In Boston on January 29, 1963

QUOTE: "A complete poem is one where an emotion has found its thought and the thought has found the words."

Note: Lines in italics are from Frost's poems: "The Pasture Spring" and "The Road Not Taken."

had a promising future in the field. Still, he was not satisfied. He wanted his poetry, not just his teaching, to be admired. He wanted to publish poems that would last through the ages. He wanted poetry to be his life's work. Frost packed up his family and sailed for England. He intended to find time and focus, to live fully the life of a poet.

Two roads diverged in a yellow wood,
And sorry I could not travel both

In England, Frost set to work revising and organizing his files of poetry. By 1913 his first collection, *A Boy's Will*, was published; a year later, a second volume, *North of Boston*, followed. The British reviews were positive, and American publishers took note. The New York firm of Henry Holt rushed to publish editions of the two volumes. By the time the Frost family returned to the United States in 1915, Robert Frost was welcomed home as a literary star.

And be one traveler, long I stood
And looked down one as far as I could

It had taken twenty years from Frost's youthful declaration to Elinor for him to produce his first published volume of poetry, but his faith in his gift had never wavered; he had never stopped writing. His first published volumes of poetry, like the later volumes, are filled with beautiful verses, many written during the years before 1913. Frost had been a poet all along, awaiting the chance to reveal himself to the literary world.

To where it bent in the undergrowth;
Then took the other, as just as fair,

Frost published thirteen additional volumes of verse and was awarded four Pulitzer Prizes. As a poet he was fascinated by the challenge of fitting the sounds, pharases, and inflections of the everyday speech of rural New Englanders to traditional meters of poetry. He wrote about the people, the

A young Robert Frost. Photo by Getty Images.

landscape, the life of rural New England, but his themes, like those of all great poetry, were universal and timeless. Frost became an American icon, the nation's most popular and widely read poet.

I took the one less traveled by,
And that has made all the difference.

One of Robert Frost's most beloved poems is about a man at a crossroads. "The Road Not Taken" is most simply and often read as a direct affirmation of the belief that the "road less traveled by" offers life's richest rewards. But an alternate reading sees that the two roads are really "worn about the same," and that the traveler's choice of path must come from within himself. This poem is not simply about which path to choose, but a reminder to choose a path deliberately and to undertake the journey without regret. This is what Frost did. He chose the path of a poet and kept to it faithfully. The rewards were rich indeed for the poet himself, and richer still for all who read and are moved by his work.

Hyla Brook
Robert Frost

By June our brook's run out of song and speed.
Sought for much after that, it will be found
Either to have gone groping underground
(And taken with it all the Hyla breed
That shouted in the mist a month ago,
Like ghost of sleigh-bells in a ghost of snow)—
Or flourished and come up in jewel-weed,
Weak foliage that is blown upon and bent
Even against the way its waters went.
Its bed is left a faded paper sheet
Of dead leaves stuck together by the heat—
A brook to none but who remember long.
This as it will be seen is other far
Than with brooks taken otherwhere in song.
We love the things we love for what they are.

*A wooden bridge crosses a small brook in
Oregon's Umpqua National Forest.
Photo by Steve Terrill.*

THE ROBERT FROST FARM
DERRY, NEW HAMPSHIRE

D. Fran Morley

Like many others, I considered a visit to the Robert Frost Farm in Derry, New Hampshire, to be a pilgrimage. Although I grew up in the Midwest, far from New England, Frost's birches and pastures, meadows and stone walls—especially the stone walls—are as clear in my mind as if I too had walked among them.

The world has changed much since 1900, the year Robert Frost and his family moved to this small farm in south New Hampshire. Today, although the farm is just a short drive away from the metro Boston area, it is still surrounded by the pastures, fields, and trees that Frost immortalized. A winding, two-lane road leads from Derry to the farm, where it is not difficult to conjure up the life and times of America's greatest poet.

The rambling old farmhouse, a simple white clapboard structure, looks much as it did when Robert and Elinor Frost and their children lived here. The home was acquired by the state and it was designated as a National Historic Landmark in the early 1960s.

My tour began with a stop at the barn that now serves as a museum and welcome center. I sat on a rustic bench, surrounded by Frost family photos, and watched a short video of Frost's life that also featured dramatic representations of his more well-known poems. Frost did not enjoy any financial success from his orchards and chickens, but he was content with life on the little farm. He would later recall his decade there as among the happiest in his life. He drew inspiration from this time for many poems, and he frequently returned to the area in his imagination.

The tour guide led our group into the house and explained how Frost's oldest daughter, Lesley, helped collect furniture of the period and style that had been in the home when she was a child. Some objects were donated by neighbors, such as kitchen gadgets and decorative items, but I was happy to learn that the lovely set of dishes displayed in the dining room had belonged to the family.

The home displays a well-known photo of Robert Frost seated in a Morris chair (a wood frame chair with padded seat and back, designed to recline in several positions). In the picture, Frost is writing on a simple board desk that he placed across the arms of the chair. Today, that chair sits in the parlor; its significance to Frost is obvious when one considers how few other original items had been retained by the family.

One surprise in the home was the telephone. I hadn't expected such a modern convenience in a rural nineteenth-century home, but Frost was fascinated by scientific inventions. Although money was tight for Frost at this time, he paid to have a telephone line run to the farm. In an odd

It shall be no trespassing
If I come again some spring
In the grey disguise of years,
Seeking ache of memory here.

juxtaposition, the kitchen remained firmly rooted in the nineteenth century—a big cast iron wood stove used for heating and cooking and no electricity. The Frosts drew water, one pail at a time, from a well outside the back door.

Attached to the small, two-story home is a series of smaller structures. These included a summer kitchen, an enclosed woodshed, and an enclosed outhouse.

After completing my tour of the home, I took a short stroll on the Hyla Brook Trail, named after Frost's beloved poem: "Hyla Brook." The quarter-mile trail winds through a field, past Frost's famous "mending wall," and along the edge of the woods. The wall of lichen-covered piled stones looked in fine shape, and I surmised that some "good neighbor" was still mending it. Hyla Brook was barely a trickle; it only runs after a New England spring rain. Details like that now seem as significant to me as they were to Frost; and as I walked along, I continued to read Frost's poetry as well as the farm's descriptions in the trail brochure and on markers.

Like a farmer harvesting his fields, Frost gathered and stored away images of Derry and the New Hampshire countryside. To some people, the area might seem to be simple farmland and somewhat uninspiring; but Frost remembered the beauty of the simple farm, and he looked beyond the ordinary to explore the very essence of life lived on a small New Hampshire farm.

Before leaving the Robert Frost Farm, I reflected on the words to the poem "On the Sale of My Farm," in which Robert Frost wrote, "It shall be no trespassing/ If I come again some spring/ In the grey disguise of years,/ Seeking ache of memory here." I don't know if Frost ever returned here; but through reading his poetry, I know he kept in his heart the "ache of memory" for his farm.

The Robert Frost Farm, Derry, New Hampshire. Photo by NH State Parks/Mary Chase.

Cowbells

Anne Campbell

We find in music universal speech;
We understand the plaintive violin.
Sweet harmony will put us within reach
Of heaven's gate and pull our spirit in.
The harp's celestial chords soothe woeful hearts.
Piano music makes our shoulders sway.
It's easier to act our little parts
With strains of music running through the day.

There is remembered music for us too,
Who have grown old and weary of the town.
Upon a vine-clad porch when day was through
We briefly sat and laid our troubles down.
The locust branches by the breeze were stirred;
Across the silver creek the fields were fair.
How soft the lowing of the lazy herd,
The cowbells ringing on the twilight air!

*Holstein cows graze on California's Sutter
Butte. Photo by Dennis Frates.*

VINTAGE FARM TOYS

Laurie Hunter

I am a transplant from rural Texas, where I was born and raised, to the city of Atlanta, Georgia. Texas had a great influence on my life, since my earliest experiences centered around the vast farmlands. When we moved to Atlanta, all things became metropolitan. Afternoons were spent at the mall, not on the ranch. Extracurricular activities included piano lessons and track meets rather than cleaning barn stalls. Breakfasts of fresh sausage and grits gave way to bagels, croissants, and biscotti. By the time I was twenty, one might not have suspeccted I had ever saddled a horse or harrowed a field.

When I had children of my own, I realized that I wanted to share with them both the leisurely pace of my childhood and the culture of my metropolitan teenage years. This desire sparked both a move to a small town on the outskirts of a large city and the idea to collect vintage farm toys for my children. Now, some six years later, my kids and I have around thirty farm toys displayed on a shelf encircling the playroom—subtle hints that our suburban lifestyle is really "down-home-on-the-farm" at heart.

I found our first collectible farm toy at a roadside flea market. The toy mechanical tractor with a red seat brought back the sense of wheat fields and long, straight dirt roads. The toy came with attachments that included a wagon, a rake, and a harrow. Its wind-up spring mechanism allows the tractor to run straight or round in circles. We placed the tractor on the bookshelf in my young son's room.

We found our next farm toy in a dusty general store in the middle of nowhere, where a tin mule caught our eyes. The toy was in its original packaging. I paid more for it than I wanted to; but it is just so different from any toy available today that I knew my children would be as fascinated with it as I was. "Jenny the Balking Mule" featured an old farmer riding a cart from which dangled a bucket of feed. The bucket hung from a long pole and dangled right in front of the mule's nose. I don't know if the wind-up mechanism works or not. I can't bring myself to break open its dusty, though cheerfully decorated, packaging.

When I saw a cast-iron, gold-colored, cow-shaped bank I recalled fondly the days of feeding the cows on the ranch. The cow bank had that same commanding look on its face as Granddaddy's cows, which implied that I should just set the feed bucket down and slowly back away. For a city girl trying to enlighten her children about life in the country, the cow bank, with its realistic udder and soft-looking nose, seemed perfect.

My favorite antique farm toy is a wind-up pig pulling a two-wheeled cart. I don't know if it's the colorful pink and red lithography, the fact that it's worth more than one thousand dollars, or its life-like, comical skipping movement when the cart is drawn along that makes the toy so endearing. I keep it prominently positioned in front of the others; the youthful pep in its step reminds me to strive for the same.

As my kids play computer games, dozens of farm toys from generations past stand sentry on the shelves of the playroom, reflecting the comfortable balance we have attained. Old-fashioned childish playthings are still right at home within today's city limits. And when I see our collection of antique farm toys, I can't help but be reminded of my early days in Texas on my Granddaddy's ranch. Sure, I got hot and filthy and tired out there on the ranch in the blazing Texas heat, but my experiences are the stuff of which memories are made.

FARM TOY COLLECTION

If you are interested in collecting vintage farm toys, the following information may be helpful.

FARM TOY MANIA

• Farm toy collecting really became popular in the late 1970s when farm toy shows became commonplace. Today, Iowa is home to the National Farm Toy Show, held the first full weekend in November, and the Summer Farm Toy Show, held the first weekend in June.

An antique pull toy from the 1800s. Photo by Jessie Walker.

• Many collectors look for farm toys that represent real machinery they have used on their own farm or toys like those they played with as children.

• Some collectors seek only the most desirable and valuable farm toys available on the market, such as vintage pieces and highly detailed, handmade items.

TYPES OF FARM TOYS TO COLLECT

Your collection of vintage farm toys might include:

• Tractors
• Implements
• Trucks
• Miniature farm scenes
• Farm machinery
• Wind-up toys
• Cast-iron toys
• Transportation toys
• Games
• Stuffed farm toys
• Popular character toys
• Banks (still or mechanical)
• Metal lithographed toys
• Celluloid or rubber toys
• Books
• Paper and wood toys

WHAT'S IT WORTH?

• Many vintage farm toys still populate the market today, including wind-up toys, stuffed nursery toys, and painted tin farm equipment.

• Prices can start at about fifteen or twenty dollars and escalate to more than fifteen hundred dollars, depending on the condition of the toy and rarity of design.

• Nostalgic appeal also plays a role in determining the price of a piece. A novelty farm toy featuring a popular character may be priced significantly higher than a comparably designed toy featuring a generic cowboy.

• The age of a toy can often be determined by the type of material used to manufacture it. Painted tin toys were made from 1840 to 1900. Cast-iron toys were manufactured from 1870 to 1930. Celluloid toys were all the rage between 1905 and 1930. Lithographed tin became popular from 1940 to 1960.

• If a farm toy is in good condition, or if it has its original label or box, its value increases. When buying toys as an investment, also remember to make sure the paint is original and that there are no missing pieces or broken parts.

INCONSISTENCY

Hazel J. Fristad

When I was a kid and I lived on the farm,
'Twas never considered the least bit of harm
To take the big rope when the haying was done
And make us a swing, for 'twas glorious fun
To swing from the rafters and out the barn doors.
And Dad didn't care when he did the barn chores
If from the high beams we all jumped to the hay,
For it was considered a tame way to play.

We waded the brooks and we tickled the frogs
And Mom didn't care if we caught polliwogs.
We climbed all the trees in the woods that we knew;
In fact, there were few things we kids didn't do.
So now, as my children are trying to swing
Inside of a little old citified thing,
I feel quite ashamed as I hear myself cry,
"Look out, oh, my dears, and don't swing it so high!"

74

Cattails border a farm pond in rural Hartford, Vermont.
Photo by William H. Johnson.

Bits and Pieces

Real beauty is in the country;
Old hills possess a charm.
In green meadows, hayracks stand
Beside an old red barn.

—*Mary Ann Putnam*

Let the farmer forevermore be honored in his calling, fo[r]
they who labor in the earth are the chosen people of Go[d.]

—*Thomas Jefferson*

Agriculture not only gives
to a nation, but the only ric[h]
she can call her own.

—*Samuel Johns*[on]

If country life be healthful
to the body, it is no less
so to the mind.

—*Giovanni Ruffini*

I love to sing of country ways
And roads that thread the scene,
The little land that idly strays
Along the village green.
—*A. S. King*

*T*he country is both the philosopher's garden and his library, in which he reads and contemplates the power, wisdom, and goodness of God.
—*William Penn*

*H*ow pleasant when the chores are done
To lie upon the hay
And hear the tranquil sounds throughout
A peaceful country day.
—*Kathleen R. Pawley*

*H*ow blessed is he who leads a country life,
Unvexed with anxious cares, and void of strife!
—*John Dryden*

*M*en are taught virtue and a love of independence by living in the country.
—*Menander*

Locust Trees

Samuel Schierloh

I never hear the poets sing
About a locust tree,
But that young grove is whispering
The dearest songs to me.

The bards have sung of hoary oaks
Withstanding years of storm,
But locust trees are like the folks
Whose simple hearts are warm.

Here, there, and everywhere they stand,
On hill and meadow's edge,
I almost feel their welcoming hand
Before I gain the ridge.

"We're just plain trees," they seem to say,
"We're not much to the eye,
It's little shade we give in May,
And little in July."

But give me just a grassy plot
Beneath such friendly shade;
I'll gather sonnets from the spot
Where locust leaves have played.

Locust blooms dangle from a tree near Taylorsville,
North Carolina. Photo by Norman Poole.

From My Garden Journal

COSMOS

Laurie Hunter

To the untrained eye, a garden might appear as if it sprang up effortlessly, like magic. True gardeners, however, know the work that is involved to create an enchanting garden. But planting flowers within the *Cosmos* genus is a bit of an exception; they will give you immediate beauty without a lot of fuss.

When we moved into our new home in Leiper's Fork, Tennessee, I turned to the cosmos for instant color and I set out a bevy of cosmos that would bring a delicate beauty to one corner of the yard and give me beautiful subjects for my watercolor painting.

Cosmos reach a height of two to six feet, so it's no sur- prise that this annual is a relative of the sunflower. Cosmos plants grow quickly to that height; and with their fine, feathery leaves and huge, daisy-like blooms that spread two to four inches in width, cosmos will add graceful height and striking beauty to any garden. And because

> As its name implies, cosmos encompasses several varieties of ethereal flowering plants that multiply as plentifully as the stars in the night sky.

they bloom from midsummer to the first frost, cosmos will add beauty all summer long with radiant white, pink, lavender, crimson, or orange blossoms.

Some Theories as to Origins of Name

Some say this flower gets its name from the Greek word *kosmos*, which means beauty. Another theory is that a field of cosmos glows with beauty like the infinite stars in the universe. Either way, as its name implies, cosmos encompasses several varieties of ethereal flowering plants that multiply as plentifully as the stars in the night sky.

Cosmos plants are members of the *Asteraceae* (*Compositae*) family. Some of the

COSMOS

most popular varieties of cosmos include Early Wonder, which flowers earlier than other cosmos, and Seashell, which blooms in gorgeous shades of pink and white petals rolled to resemble delicate conch shells. Candy Stripe, as you may guess, sports white flowers with crimson borders. Sonata, a good choice for a small garden, is a white dwarf cosmos that only grows two to two and a half feet tall. For a bushier plant, try the tall, lush strain called Purity. Versailles Pink Eye grows on thick, sturdy stems; its pale pink flowers with dark centers are pleasing in a cut-flower bouquet. Sensation Mixed is another good choice, growing four-inch-wide flowers in white, pink, rose, or crimson.

The Need for Support

To provide strength to my cosmos plants on windy days, I plant them near a garden fence or stake the growing blooms in my children's garden. The children love the butterflies and birds that the towering beauties attract. My children are also pleased with how quickly the cosmos grows. In the past, I have tried to make my cosmos appear more natural by scattering them in a grassy area of my backyard. This effort was in vain, however, because the wildflowers were tougher and eventually crowded out the roots of cosmos.

Plant Once, Enjoy for Years

Cosmos is self-sowing and will most likely only need planting once. The seeds may be planted indoors in spring and transplanted to the garden a few weeks prior to summer; they may also be planted outdoors after the ground is warm. To get started, prepare the soil in a section of your garden that receives full sun. Sow seeds after all danger of frost has passed, typi-

cally in March or April. When the plants have grown to a height of one to one and a half feet, pinch off the stem tips to encourage the plant to branch out and create more blooms.

Because cosmos plants were brought to the United States from Mexico, they can, therefore, tolerate dry soil and hot climates, even drought. For the best growth and most prolific flowering, however, water your cosmos regularly.

The Cosmos Has Many Fans

Cosmos is a favored flower in Japan. In Iizuka City, six hundred meters of cosmos flowers are planted every year and line a grass-covered parkway where families and visitors gather to stroll and enjoy the blooms. The cosmos has endeared itself to me too and, in fact, is now one of my favorite varieties of flowers. From an artist's perspective, a cosmos bloom looks like the skirt of a delicate bridal gown topped by a fairy's crown of tightly woven golden blooms and beads. And once I became a cosmos fancier, I found that these flowers were featured in numerous famous paintings and several unknown sketches of my own.

Once the cosmos seedlings in my garden began to bloom, I found an old wooden church pew that was painted a weathered grass green and placed it among the plants. This corner of the garden is now a space in which to be quiet, appreciate solitude, rest beneath fluttering plumes of petals, and soak in the magical qualities of a light-hearted patch of cosmos.

Laurie Hunter lives with her family in Leiper's Fork, Tennessee, where young Alexis and Oliver love to follow her through the garden.

A Summer Day

Alfred Ebelt

What is more inspiring
Than to waken in the morn
And view the golden sunrise
When a summer day is born?
To stroll out in the meadow
When the grass is wet with dew
And all the birds and flowers
Seem to say good morn to you?
To take your rod and reel and sit
Beside a quiet stream
And harken to its murmur
While you tarry there and dream?
To wander in the woodland
As you wend your homeward way,
Admiring this masterpiece—
A perfect summer day?
To linger on the doorstep
At the home you love so well
And watch the crimson sunset
As it casts a magic spell?
What is more enchanting
Than to rest there in the eve
While the shadows lengthen
And a summer day takes leave?

These beautiful days most enrich all my life. They do not exist as mere pictures, maps hung upon the walls of memory. But they saturate themselves into every part of the body and live always.

—John Muir

A country garden overflows with cosmos and snapdragons in Bristol, New Hampshire. Photo by William H. Johnson.

83

HOLY PLACES

Berta Hull Coon

Late July, and early morning,
Road a beck'ning, wheedling thing,
Mystery lies beyond the bend;
Dipping, circling air-tribes sing;
Color splotches twixt bleached boulders;
Brown-eyed Susans, stately, tall;
Queen Anne's lace, in dainty clusters;
Goldenrod 'gainst yonder wall;
Late wild roses, fragrant, nodding;
Marsh, a red and yellow mass;

Each flower vying, gaily waving
Glad "good morning" as we pass;
And above the wooded hillside
Where staid cattle graze, by day,
Gleam the spires of village churches
Calling some indoors to pray.
God of flowers and field and wood,
Tune our hearts to what is good,
Whether we in "closet" pray,
Or mid fields and flowers stray.

Bluebonnets line a road in the hill country of Texas. Photo by Dick Dietrich.

Readers' Forum

Snapshots from our IDEALS Readers

Top: Little Kelly Hodges shows off her grin and her two-and-a-half-pound tomato. She is the daughter of Patrick and Jennifer Hodges of Nampa, Idaho.

Below left: Jesse and Jacob Jacobusse, age three, share a swing and a memory. The twins are the great-grandchildren of Iva Stassen, who lives in Holland, Michigan.

Below right: Fifteen-month-old Robert C. Edwards is trying out his green thumb at an early age. Robert is the great-grandson of Virginia Jones of Blairs, Virginia.

Top: While visiting his Meme (Mary Robbins of Skippack, Pennsylvania), two-year-old Brent Horsey was thrilled to discover a "fluffy" flower.

Middle: Luke and Kathy Hermanson of Lester Prairie, Minnesota, share this photo of their granddaughter, Mariah Katherine. Three-and-a-half-year-old Mariah believes summer calls for a drink from the hose.

Below: Carol and Robert Maples of Richmond, Missouri, sent us this photo of their grandsons. Preston and Samuel Maples, ages eight and two, are sharing a summer afternoon at the fishing hole.

THANK YOU Mr. and Mrs. Hodges, Mrs. Stassen, Mrs. Jones, Mr. and Mrs. Robbins, Mr. and Mrs. Hermanson, Mr. and Mrs. Maples, Mrs. Howell, Mrs. Colello, and Mrs. Balzer for sharing your family photographs with *Ideals.* We hope to hear from other readers who would like to share snapshots with the *Ideals* family. Please include a self-addressed, stamped envelope if you would like the photos returned. Keep your original photographs for safekeeping and send duplicate photos along with your name, address, and telephone number to:

Readers' Forum
Ideals Publications
535 Metroplex Drive, Suite 250
Nashville, Tennessee 37211

ideals

Publisher, Patricia A. Pingry
Editor, Michelle Prater Burke
Managing Editor, Peggy Schaefer
Designer, Marisa Calvin
Copy Editor, Melinda Rathjen
Editorial Assistant, Patsy Jay
Contributing Editors, Lansing Christman and Pamela Kennedy

Acknowledgments

Barker, S. Omar. "God's Helper." Used by permission of Marjorie A. Phillips. Burket, Gail Brook. "The Opportunity." Used by permission of Anne E. Burket. Calvert, Catherine. "Summer Kids." Reprinted by permission of *Victoria* Magazine. Copyright © 2003 by Hearst Communications, Inc. Crowell, Grace Noll. "A Message to Fathers." Used by permission of Claire Cumberworth. Jaques, Edna. "The Farmer" from *Beside Still Waters* by Edna Jaques. Used by permission of Thomas Allen & Son, Limited, Canada. Leitner, Della Adams. "July." Used by permission of Sally Leitner. Liddell, Evelyn R. "Found: Lost Youth." Used by permission of Lori Liddell Phillips. Murton, Jessie Wilmore. "Ten Rosy Fingers." By courtesy of Pacific Press and the author's estate. Sathoff, Craig E. "Two Shadows on the Wall." Used by permission of Mary Sathoff. Scriba, Jay. "When Trail's End Was Only the Beginning" from *The Milwaukee Journal*, August 8, 1971. Copyright © 1971. Used by permission of the *Milwaukee Journal Sentinel*. Our sincere thanks to the following authors and heirs whom we were unable to locate: The Estate of Caroline Henning Bair for "June"; Berta Hull Coon for "Holy Places"; Lance Delaney for "Boy and Clover" from *Poor Richard's Anthology on Father and Son*, Shaw Publishing; The Estate of Samuel Schierloh for "Locust Trees"; Victor E. Southworth for "Know'st Thou America."

Top: At only six months of age, Eric Steven Howell knows how handsome he looks in his swimsuit. Eric's proud grandmother is Evelyn Howell of Hot Springs, Arkansas.

Middle: Young Antonio William Colello discovers the joys of the beach. The photo was sent to us by Shirley P. Colello of Steelton, Pennsylvania.

Right: With a broken leg, one-and-a-half-year-old Chaz Morgan can only watch as big sister Kaeli, age three, plays in the pool. The photo was sent to us by the siblings' grandmother, Josephine Balzer of Prairieville, Louisiana.

WARM YOUR HEART
AND LIFT YOUR SOUL . . .

As Henry Wadsworth Longfellow once wrote, poems can soothe our souls and give us rest; and, when read aloud, the cadence of their meter and the rhymes of their words lend a beautiful musical quality to the verse. But poems can also be stories, sonnets to a loved one, humorous poems that make us laugh out loud, courageous poems that inspire great deeds, or even silly rhymes we loved as children.

There are so many inspiring, wonderful, and familiar poems. Naturally, there should be one huge magnificent and colorful volume packed with the most beloved poems of all time. That volume is *THE IDEALS TREASURY OF BEST LOVED POEMS*, where you will find more than 100 poems, all of which have been carefully selected. These are the poems that have stood the test of time, that are traditional but express a feeling of emotion so powerful that reading them becomes a moment of wonder.

These are the poems you'll remember from your childhood or that you recited in your youth; some you'll discover for the first time. All will soothe, encourage, and inspire you for the rest of your life. They include lines that have raised the spirits and comforted generations of readers, and you will find yourself turning to them again and again.

Exclusive highlights—

- 160 pages, heavy-weight enamel stock, deluxe hardcover binding
- Full-color photographs throughout
- Over 100 poems
- Poems about Love, Family and Children, Nature, Courage and Faith

FREE just for ordering!

Return the Free Examination Certificate today to preview *THE IDEALS TREASURY OF BEST LOVED POEMS* for 30 days FREE . . . and receive FREE *FLORAL POSTCARDS* just for ordering.

COMPLETE THE FREE EXAMINATION CERTIFICATE AND MAIL TODAY FOR YOUR 30-DAY PREVIEW.

No need to send money now!

Spend a Day in the Life of Dearest Dorothy!

A GUIDEPOSTS Exclusive

Dearest Dorothy—She's the Dearest Woman You'll Ever Meet.

Share the humorous and true-to-life adventures of Partonville's most endearing resident in the highly engaging, two-book set. *Dearest Dorothy, Are We There Yet?* and its sequel *Dearest Dorothy, Slow Down, You're Wearing Us Out!* reflect the pace, the memories, the worries, joys and friendships of small-town America. Best of all, they'll touch your heart and tickle your funny bone at the same time!

Meet an 87-year-old "Youngster"—Full of Joy and Inspiration!

Dorothy Jean Westra has been living in perpetual fast motion for the past 87 years. And she has no intention of slowing down. Share in the delightful adventures of a remarkable, inspiring woman who turns to God, friends and her own inner-strength to triumph!

Welcome to Dorothy's World—meet the dear, fun-loving folks of Partonville.

Whether she's traveling in her battle-scarred Lincoln Continental with her sidekick Sheeba, Queen of the Mutt Dogs, or attending a Happy Hookers—they used to hook rugs—meeting, this silver-haired heroine knows how to embrace life—and so do her friends. Meet them all in this exclusive, two-book set.

Created by beloved Christian humorist Charlene Ann Baumbich, the embraceable character of Dorothy was inspired by a dear, 87-year-old friend who taught Charlene to laugh and live joyfully. Embrace the spirit of this heartwarming heroine as she struggles to serve God's children, do what's right and live every day to the fullest—pedal *down* and prayers *up*!

A Guideposts Exclusive Two-Book Set!

- Fun, prayerful adventures from beloved Christian humorist Charlene Ann Baumbich

- Two handsome, hardcover editions– over 400 pages in all!

- Actual size: 5 1/2" x 8" each

- Makes a great gift!

Take advantage of our 30-day preview without any obligation. Simply return the Free Examination Certificate and we'll send you this highly engaging two-book set to preview in the privacy of your home. When you reply today, we'll send you a FREE bonus gift — a beautiful bookmark. Yours to keep, no matter what.

To be seventy years young is sometimes far more cheerful and hopeful than to be forty years old.
—Oliver Wendell Holmes

A FREE Gift!

NO NEED TO SEND MONEY NOW!

FREE EXAMINATION CERTIFICATE

YES! Please rush me *Dearest Dorothy, Are We There Yet?* and its sequel *Dearest Dorothy, Slow Down, You're Wearing Us Out!* at no risk or obligation. If I decide to keep the two-book set, I will be billed later at the low Guideposts price of only $18.96, payable in two installments of $9.48, each plus postage and handling. If not completely satisfied, I may return the books within 30 days and owe nothing. The FREE Bookmark is mine to keep no matter what I decide.

Total sets ordered: _____

Please print your name and address:

NAME _____

ADDRESS _____ APT# _____

CITY _____ STATE _____ ZIP _____

❑ Please Bill Me ❑ Charge My: ❑ MasterCard ❑ Visa
Credit Card #:

Expiration Date: _____
Signature _____

Allow 4 weeks for delivery. Orders subject to credit approval.
Send no money now. We will bill you later.
www.guidepostsbooks.com

Printed in USA
11/202059693